MW00572404

# Paris

## by Eboni Booth

## FOR PRODUCTION INQUIRIES

UNITED STATES AND CANADA
info@concordtheatricals.com
1-866-979-0447

UNITED KINGDOM AND EUROPE
licensing@concordtheatricals.co.uk
020-7054-7298

Each title is subject to availability from Concord Theatricals Corp., depending upon country of performance. Please be aware that *PARIS* may not be licensed by Concord Theatricals Corp. in your territory. Professional and amateur producers should contact the nearest Concord Theatricals Corp. office or licensing partner to verify availability.

No one shall make any changes in this title(s) for the purpose of production. No part of this book may be reproduced, stored in a retrieval system, scanned, uploaded, or transmitted in any form, by any means, now known or yet to be invented, including mechanical, electronic, digital, photocopying, recording, videotaping, or otherwise, without the prior written permission of the publisher. No one shall share this title(s), or any part of this title(s), through any social media or file hosting websites.

For all inquiries regarding motion picture, television, online/digital and other media rights, please contact Concord Theatricals Corp.

## MUSIC AND THIRD-PARTY MATERIALS USE NOTE

Licensees are solely responsible for obtaining formal written permission from copyright owners to use copyrighted music and/or other copyrighted third-party materials (e.g., artworks, logos) in the performance of this play and are strongly cautioned to do so. If no such permission is obtained by the licensee, then the licensee must use only original music and materials that the licensee owns and controls. Licensees are solely responsible and liable for clearances of all third-party copyrighted materials, including without limitation music, and shall indemnify the copyright owners of the play(s) and their licensing agent, Concord Theatricals Corp., against any costs, expenses, losses and liabilities arising from the use of such copyrighted third-party materials by licensees. For music, please contact the appropriate music licensing authority in your territory for the rights to any incidental music.

## IMPORTANT BILLING AND CREDIT REQUIREMENTS

If you have obtained performance rights to this title, please refer to your licensing agreement for important billing and credit requirements.

*PARIS* was first produced by the Atlantic Theater Company (Neil Pepe, Artistic Director; Jeffory Lawson, Managing Director) in New York, New York on January 8, 2020. The performance was directed by Knud Adams, with sets by David Zinn, costumes by Arnulfo Maldonado, lights by Oona Curley, sound by Fan Zhang, wig, hair, and makeup by J. Jared Janas, with original compositions by Trey Anastasio. The production stage manager was Kristy Bodall. The cast was as follows:

**EMMIE** . . . . . . . . . . . . . . . . . . . . . . . . . . . . . . . . . . . . . . . . . . . . . Jules Latimer

**GAR** . . . . . . . . . . . . . . . . . . . . . . . . . . . . . . . . . . . . . . . . .Eddie K. Robinson

**LOGAN** . . . . . . . . . . . . . . . . . . . . . . . . . . . . . . .Christopher Dylan White

**MAXINE** . . . . . . . . . . . . . . . . . . . . . . . . . . . . . . . . . . . . .Danielle Skraastad

**WENDY** . . . . . . . . . . . . . . . . . . . . . . . . . . . . . . . . . . . . . . . Ann McDonough

**DEV** . . . . . . . . . . . . . . . . . . . . . . . . . . . . . . . . . . . . . . . . James Murtaugh

**CARLISLE** . . . . . . . . . . . . . . . . . . . . . . . . . . . . . . . . . . . . .Bruce McKenzie

# CHARACTERS

(in speaking order)

**EMMIE** – female, early twenties, black

**GAR** – male, thirties to forties, black

**LOGAN** – male, early twenties, white

**MAXINE** – female, late-thirties to forties, white

**WENDY** – female, sixties to seventies, white

**DEV** – male, sixties to seventies, white

**CARLISLE** – male, forties to fifties, white


# SETTING

The breakroom and warehouse of Berry's, a large store off the interstate. Berry's sells everything from baby carrots to lawnmowers.

Paris, a small town in Vermont.

USA.


# TIME

Christmas holidays, 1995.


# AUTHOR'S NOTES

A slash ( / ) indicates overlapping text.

If the slash ( / ) appears at the start of the line, the following line should start at the same time. So for this exchange:

> **GAR.** Don't come to work drunk.
> **EMMIE.** / Okay.

Both Emmie and Gar would start speaking their lines at the same time.

*For Hope*

# One

*(The windowless breakroom of Berry's, a large "everything store" just south of Route 4 in Paris, Vermont.)*

*(The walls are covered in holiday decorations. A plastic Christmas tree sits in the corner.)*

*(**EMMIE** watches an animated orientation video on a large TV as she fills out a job application.)*

*(The right side of her face is badly scraped and very, very swollen. She holds a napkin to the corner of her mouth to catch any dribble.)*

**ORIENTATION VIDEO.** *(Voiceover.)* ...but then there was the agricultural revolution, which sent thousands of hardworking farm folks in search of a paycheck! And not in the form of welfare dollars or government handouts! These Americans wanted good, honest, old-fashioned work! That's where Berry's stepped in!

We want to forge –

We want to forge –

> *(The orientation tape jams and begins to warble.)*

We want to forge a durable connection with our employees.

One rooted in trust, hard work, and an abiding faith in our ability to turn raw material into market power.

*(Music\*.)*

Here at Berry's, we believe it is our duty to celebrate diversity and honor the many voices that contribute to America's glory. But we also want a workforce that is uniformly diligent, and should you come across anyone trying to unionize –

*(The music\* changes. Drums beat ominously.)*

– or organize team members with methods that don't appear in the Berry's Employee Handbook, you should notify management immediately. Once, many many many years ago, unions had a place in American society. But as more worker-friendly companies like Berry's emerged, unions became obsolete!

*(The drums ends.)*

So welcome to the family! We hope this orientation has given you everything you need to get started at Vermont's number one storeway to heaven! And remember, the best ideas come from our associates, so we look forward to hearing from YOU about how we can continue to grow, prosper, and keep our aisles stocked with pieces of the American dream.

*(Music fades out.)*

*(**EMMIE** finishes her application.)*

*(The video screen fades to blue. Static. Video out.)*

*(**GAR** comes back into the breakroom.)*

**GAR.** Yup?

---

\* A license to produce *Paris* does not include a performance license for any third-party or copyrighted music. Licensees should create an original composition or use music in the public domain. For further information, please see the Music and Third Party Materials Use Note on page iii.

**EMMIE.** I think so.

*(He reaches for her application on the table.)*

**GAR.** I'll take that.

Are you cold?

**EMMIE.** No.

**GAR.** You look cold.

**EMMIE.** I'm okay.

*(He looks at her.)*

*(She looks at him.)*

**GAR.** *(Looking at her application.)* So what do you think?

**EMMIE.** I think it's great. The tape was really informative.

**GAR.** Seem like a good place to work?

**EMMIE.** It does. Definitely.

**GAR.** Favorite Talking Heads song.

**EMMIE.** What?

**GAR.** Go.

**EMMIE.** Oh.

**GAR.** Mine is "Road to Nowhere."

**EMMIE.** / Ummm –

**GAR.** Clock's ticking. You want this job or not?

**EMMIE.** Uh – "Go Your Own Way."

No – "The Chain."

**GAR.** Those are Fleetwood Mac songs. / Thanks for coming in.

**EMMIE.** No no no, let me try again.

**GAR.**  Just kidding. Relax. Just having some fun, I like to add personal touches to my interviews. Make sure you can think on your feet. That'll be an important part of the job, of being out on the floor.

**EMMIE.**  I can do it.

**GAR.**  What did you study at –

*(He looks down at his clipboard.)*

**EMMIE.**  I went for a year. But I didn't finish.

**GAR.**  Down in Maryland?

**EMMIE.**  It's in DC.

**GAR.**  I'm from Richmond.

**EMMIE.**  Oh.

Okay.

**GAR.**  I think my friend went there. You know Nathan? Pearce?

**EMMIE.**  I don't think so.

**GAR.**  Good buddy of mine, great guy. You should look him up.

*(Back to his clipboard.)*

So you already have a job now?

**EMMIE.**  I do. I work nights as a waitress over at Blonde Jovi. They have really fun karaoke on the weekends –

**GAR.**  Yeah, I know it.

**EMMIE.**  – but I have a lot of flexibility and your ad said you were looking for daytime stockers, and I've done it before, had two jobs, and I don't get tired or lose stamina, and I know how to manage my time and maintain my energy.

**GAR.**  Yeah, you wrote that down here.

**EMMIE.** I also have references from –

**GAR.** Yup, I see them.

**EMMIE.** Sorry.

**GAR.** You're fine.

**EMMIE.** I've been applying a lot of places. / I'm on autopilot.

**GAR.** Tip for the future? When you're interviewing for one job, don't talk about the other jobs / you want.

**EMMIE.** Oh, no no, I want to work here – I just –

**GAR.** Where else did you apply?

**EMMIE.** Uh – Pick a Dollar.

**GAR.** Uh-huh.

**EMMIE.** Krabby Patty's.

Funky Friday's, Hobo Billy's, Fat Willie's. All those restaurants and hotels along 68.

**GAR.** Did you apply to Price Chopper?

**EMMIE.** Yeah. Like a week ago.

**GAR.** Uh-huh.

**EMMIE.** But.

**GAR.** They won't let you work the register.

**EMMIE.** She said I could only work in the meat room.

**GAR.** Yeah, they did that to me, too. They're fucks, pardon my language, but I wrote four letters to corporate. They'll get theirs.

*(A knock on the breakroom door.)*

*(DEV pokes his head in.)*

**DEV.** Knock knock knockie, a Merry Christmas and Happy New Year to you all!

GAR.  Not a good time.

> (**DEV** *enters carrying two cardboard boxes of books.*)

DEV.  Now I know you told me to wait until after the holidays –

GAR.  Yes, I did tell you that.

DEV.  – and I know how to follow rules – I respect your authority – but I couldn't let you miss out on this offer of a lifetime. What kind of friend would I be / if I didn't help you nab an offer of a lifetime?

GAR.  We're not friends. Don't unpack those.

> (**DEV** *starts to open his boxes and take out the books.*)

DEV.  *(To* **EMMIE**.*)* Hi honey, you looking for a job?

GAR.  Listen –

DEV.  No, you listen. Listen, listen.

Two platforms. Right by the main entrance. Forty books. I'll give them to you sixty on the dollar.

GAR.  I already told you. This needs to go through corporate.

DEV.  Who doesn't need to learn about money management this time of year?

*(To* **EMMIE**.*)* Honey, you know who Jason Juno is?

EMMIE.  I don't.

> (**DEV** *takes a book out of the box, hands it to* **EMMIE**.*)*

DEV.  *The Magic Money Maven*?

*Move Out of the Way, Let Your Money Have a Say*?

You read these books, you won't need this job here.

**GAR.** Dev, / get out.

**DEV.** *(Handing* **EMMIE** *a business card.)* Take my card. If he doesn't hire you, come work for me. It's part-time work, full-time pay. You buy forty books, sell them within the month, advance to the next level. What were you making on your last job?

**GAR.** I'm calling security.

**DEV.** *(Packing up his things.)* Okay okay okay, I gotta get back to the station anyway. Tell Wendy I'll be by to pick her up at eight. And Gar.

Think about it.

Everybody wants to change their lives this time of year. Shouldn't Berry's be the one place in town to help them do that? Don't say no to free money! Honey, call me and keep my card. Merry Christmas.

*(***DEV*** exits.)*

*(***GAR*** slams the door behind him.)*

*(Back to his clipboard.)*

**GAR.** Why do you want to work at Berry's?

**EMMIE.** Ummm, I want – I want to be part of a hardworking team that's focused on customer service.

**GAR.** Uh-huh.

Do you work well with others?

**EMMIE.** I do.

**GAR.** Are you prone to moods of self-pity?

*(***EMMIE*** looks at him.)*

**EMMIE.** I'm – not.

**GAR.** Is management to blame if things go wrong?

EMMIE. No.

GAR. What should you do if an unforeseen conflict arises at work?

EMMIE. Well, I think I'm pretty good with troubleshooting.

So if an issue did arise, I think I would know how to handle it.

GAR. Wrong answer.

If there is ever a conflict, you come get a manager.

EMMIE. Oh, right.

GAR. That's why we're here. It's what we're trained for.

EMMIE. Okay.

GAR. I started like you, I was an associate and thought I could handle anything that came my way. But after being a higher-up for close to nine months now, I can see the gaps in my knowledge.

You have to rely on the management team.

EMMIE. Yes. If I – if I get hired, I will rely on you.

GAR. I can't put you on the floor with your face like that. You would have to work the stockroom or warehouse.

EMMIE. I fell at work, I hit the ice in the parking lot –

GAR. Okay. Not my business.

EMMIE. – but I thought I'd be healed by the time –

I didn't realize the interview process was so quick.

GAR. Will your drug test come back clean?

EMMIE. Yes.

They're – yes, clean. I mentioned I'm taking pain medication but –

(*A knock on the door.* LOGAN *enters.*)

**LOGAN.** How now, brother?

**GAR.** Did you see the door was closed?

**LOGAN.** That guy is here to see you.

**GAR.** A closed door means the breakroom is unavailable.

**LOGAN.** That guy is here to see you.

**GAR.** If you can't follow the rules, Logan, I'll be happy to let corporate know.

**LOGAN.** That guy is here to see you.

**GAR.** Get out.

**LOGAN.** *(To* **EMMIE.***)* Jesus Christ, what the fuck happened to your face?

**GAR.** If you don't get back to the floor –

**LOGAN.** *(To* **EMMIE.***)* Leave him, honey, no man is worth that.

**GAR.** – I'll make sure you never work Electronics again.

**LOGAN.** *(To* **EMMIE.***)* Make sure to ask about overtime.

**GAR.** Get out.

**LOGAN.** *(To* **EMMIE.***)* And get a free tote bag.

> *(He leaves.)*

> **(GAR** *slams the door behind* **LOGAN.** *He opens it and slams it once more.)*

> *(He turns back to* **EMMIE.***)*

**GAR.** We do have day shifts, but if I need you for nights, you have to find a way to make yourself available.

**EMMIE.** Am I hired?

**GAR.** No visible tattoos, no ripped jeans. Every employee must wear deodorant.

**EMMIE.**  Okay.

**GAR.**  No face jewelry.

**EMMIE.**  Okay.

**GAR.**  Don't come to work drunk.

**EMMIE.**  / Okay.

**GAR.**  *If* you're hired, you must wear rubber-soled shoes at all times, and carry a knife and/or box cutter. If you don't own these items, you can purchase them from Berry's and we'll deduct the cost from your first paycheck.

**EMMIE.**  / Okay.

**GAR.**  Security will check your bags at the beginning and end of every shift.

**EMMIE.**  That's – fine.

**GAR.**  There is no overtime pay.

**EMMIE.**  Okay.

**GAR.**  No holiday bonuses.

**EMMIE.**  Okay.

**GAR.**  You sure want this job?

**EMMIE.**  I –

> *(A moment.)*

Yes. I do.

> *(He checks his clipboard.)*

**GAR.**  Do you go by Emmie or Emaani?

**EMMIE.**  Whichever. Both.

Mostly Emmie.

**GAR.**  Muslim?

EMMIE.  My mother.

> *(He goes to a closet and gets two bright red employee vests.)*

I'm sorry, does this mean I'm hired?

> *(He goes to a little printing machine and types. And ID badge spits out.)*

> *(He types again and a second badge prints.)*

GAR.  I made you two. One with each name, you can decide which you want to use. Or wear a different one each day.

> *(He hands EMMIE her vests and badges.)*

EMMIE.  Thank you. That's – that's very thoughtful.

GAR.  We'll start you at five dollars an hour.

EMMIE.  Oh my god. Really?

GAR.  I told you: we care about our employees at Berry's.

EMMIE.  Holy crap – excuse me, I mean –

I've been looking for weeks now and –

> *(A moment.)*

It's really good to find something. Thank you. And I really, really do want to work here.

GAR.  You're happy.

EMMIE.  I'm happy.

GAR.  Good. You can start training tomorrow. Seven a.m. sharp. Find Otis in the warehouse.

> *(He collects his things.)*

Welcome to the family.

*(Lights shift.)*

(**EMMIE** *exits.)*

(**GAR** *sits at the breakroom table.)*

## Two

*(Four days later. In the warehouse. The distant sound of holiday music\* piping through the speakers in the store.)*

*(EMMIE unpacks boxes and tags bright yellow sweatshirts.)*

*(She is listening to a Walkman clipped to her belt.)*

*(MAXINE and LOGAN come through the warehouse's swinging doors.)*

**MAXINE.** But I'm not talking about that, I'm talking about respect.

**LOGAN.** I hear you.

**MAXINE.** One minute.

**LOGAN.** I know.

**MAXINE.** One goddamned minute. How do they expect me to live? This isn't about the rules anymore, Logan, this is an issue of –

**LOGAN.** I hear you.

**MAXINE.** Decency. / Morality. Virtue.

**LOGAN.** I'm right here with you, girl.

**MAXINE.** And it really fucking grinds my gears because they say they want us to maintain dignity – well, they don't say that, they don't fucking say that, but it's how they act in the videos and then they treat us like trash,

---

\* A license to produce *Paris* does not include a performance license for any third-party or copyrighted music. Licensees should create an original composition or use music in the public domain. For further information, please see the Music and Third Party Materials Use Note on page iii.

like goddamned trash, all this "family" bullcrap, but you're not supposed to treat your "family" like that, are you? Are you??

LOGAN.  In my family, you can get away with it.

MAXINE.  You know, I'm not scared to say it, Logan – I'm talking about ethics.

LOGAN.  That's a big word, Max.

MAXINE.  It is! It is a big word and they'll be hearing it down at the newspaper when I start whistleblowing like an asshole around here because when you have four kids and get docked for going one minute over on your bathroom break –

LOGAN.  One minute.

MAXINE.  One fuckface minute over, people are going to hear about it. The public needs to know. You don't think I can make heads roll?

LOGAN.  I absolutely think you can make heads roll.

MAXINE.  This whole operation will be going fucking bye-bye because I have to be able to use the bathroom and it shouldn't be fucking timed because you need to hydrate when you're standing on your feet all day – that requires energy and water is life and you need it to live and I'm not even drinking vodka out of a water bottle like Peggy, I'm drinking so I can get my electrolytes and I'm sorry if we can't all pee in one point five fucking minutes –

LOGAN.  Are you kidding me? It takes me three point five fucking minutes, and that's / just for number one.

MAXINE.  Exactly! Exactly. It takes more time to care for yourself and the next time I have to pee, I'll just do it right there in Housewares so I don't eat up my break walking to and from the fucking bathroom, I'll just pull my pussy out in front of the vacuum cleaners and the customers and their kids and everyone will be able to see my vagina, nothing will be hidden because what little pubic hair I had left has fallen out from the stress of this job.

LOGAN. They need to learn.

MAXINE. I have a Scorpio moon.

LOGAN. They gotta do better.

MAXINE. Gar won't even look me in the *fucking* eye.

*(Talking to the imaginary villain in her mind.)* Well just come for me and see what I can do. Just come and try to find me and and and –

*(LOGAN comforts MAXINE. She is very upset.)*

LOGAN. Okay okay, come on, it's okay. You're okay.

MAXINE. Let them find me and see what I'm made of. Let them –

*(She catches EMMIE staring at her.)*

What are you staring at?

EMMIE. Sorry.

*(EMMIE tries to go back to work.)*

MAXINE. You want to see what I'm made of?

EMMIE. No. Thank you. I'm sorry.

*(MAXINE stands in EMMIE's face.)*

MAXINE. Stop fucking looking at me.

EMMIE. Okay.

MAXINE. Stop fucking looking! Don't look at me! Don't look at me! Don't fucking look at me!

*(She slams out of the swinging doors.)*

(**EMMIE** *is shaken.*)

(*A moment.*)

**LOGAN.**  She's got four kids and lives in the hotel behind Costco.

Don't take it personally.

(*He lights a cigarette.*)

(**EMMIE** *looks at him and his rule breaking.*)

It's cool. I have friends in corporate.

(*She gets back to work.* **LOGAN** *watches her.*)

Are you doing that right?

**EMMIE.**  I think so.

**LOGAN.**  Okay.

**EMMIE.**  Otis said to enter each number.

**LOGAN.**  Okay.

**EMMIE.**  Print the labels.

**LOGAN.**  Okay.

**EMMIE.**  Is that wrong?

**LOGAN.**  No.

You should listen to Otis.

(*He smokes. She keeps working.*)

You want a cigarette?

**EMMIE.**  I don't smoke.

**LOGAN.**  Why not?

**EMMIE.**  Because they're bad for your health.

**LOGAN.**  Says who?

**EMMIE.** I'm not judging you.

**LOGAN.** No, I'm just curious where you get your information.

**EMMIE.** From every doctor in the country.

**LOGAN.** My grandmother says that might be a conspiracy.

**EMMIE.** Yeah, my mother said that too.

**LOGAN.** See?

**EMMIE.** And she smoked two packs of cigarettes every day until she died.

**LOGAN.** Uh-huh.

**EMMIE.** Of lung cancer.

**LOGAN.** Gotcha.

**EMMIE.** So I don't smoke.

**LOGAN.** Right.

*(A moment.)*

What about weed?

**EMMIE.** *(Re: the sweatshirts.)* I should get back to doing these.

**LOGAN.** *(Re: her Walkman.)* What are you listening to?

**EMMIE.** Blues Traveler.

**LOGAN.** Ew.

**EMMIE.** I like them.

**LOGAN.** I like Wu-Tang.

You know them? You like them? The Wu-Tang Clan?

**EMMIE.** I've heard of them.

**LOGAN.** I rap, too.

I'm in a band.

A rap band.

The Enemy Boyz. You ever heard of us?

We got our first show coming up.

**EMMIE.** Good for you.

**LOGAN.** You should come.

**EMMIE.** Okay.

**LOGAN.** Playing up in Burlington, open mic night. Next week. You and friends, come check it out.

**EMMIE.** Okay.

> *(He smokes and then kind of starts rap-singing.)*

**LOGAN.** *(Rapping.)*
I'M COMING FOR YO FACE
I'M ALL UP IN YO NECK
TELL THE BIG BOYZ THEY BETTER WRITE THAT CHECK!
WHO'S KNOWING HOW TO GO?
WHICH WAY YOU GONNA TURN?
WATCH OUT MOTHERFUCKA, 'FO YO ASS GETS BURNED
URBAN FIST! STREET POWER! ALL UP IN MY CRIB!
CHILL WITH THAT, RELAX, WHILE I SHARPEN THIS SHIV.

> *(A moment.)*

Yeah, I like Wu-Tang. They're from New York. I think like Staten Island?

**EMMIE.** That's cool.

**LOGAN.** Are you from New York?

**EMMIE.** I'm from Paris.

**LOGAN.** No you're not.

**EMMIE.** Yes I am.

**LOGAN.** Where'd you go to elementary school?

**EMMIE.** Wilson.

**LOGAN.** Who was your favorite gym teacher?

**EMMIE.** Mrs. Greenfield.

Duh.

**LOGAN.** Which ice cream shop has the blue clown out front? Penguin's or / Tommy's?

**EMMIE.** Tommy's.

**LOGAN.** You're not from here.

**EMMIE.** Why would I lie?

**LOGAN.** I've never seen you.

**EMMIE.** Why would I lie about being from this shitty town?

**LOGAN.** People lie all the time, girl. It's a way of life.

You're bleeding.

**EMMIE.** What?

> *(He points to her face. She has started bleeding from the swollen side of her mouth. It dribbles onto one of the sweatshirts she is tagging.)*

Oh shit. Oh no.

> *(She fumbles in her pockets for tissue, stuffs some into her bleeding cheek and tries to wipe the sweatshirt.)*

> *(The blood smears.)*

**LOGAN.** You're making it worse.

**EMMIE.** Oh fuck. Please. Shit, shit.

> *(She keeps wiping the bloody sweatshirt.)*

**LOGAN.** Okay, relax.

*(Pointing to her face.)* Why don't you handle that first?
Go clean up.

**EMMIE.**  I can't leave the floor unless I have permission
from a manager.

**LOGAN.**  Sometimes if there's blood involved they'll make
an exception.

> *(She grabs her backpack from under the
> table, taking out a little medical bag and a
> hand mirror.)*

You should really go to the bathroom and do that.

**EMMIE.**  I don't want to get in trouble.

**LOGAN.**  You'll get in more trouble for doing this. Especially
if they see you have your bag with you. Put your stuff in
your locker.

> *(She crouches near the table and cleans her
> face.)*

Maybe you need to go to the doctor.

**EMMIE.**  I already went to the doctor.

**LOGAN.**  Maybe you need to go again.

> *(She cleans up the bloody tissue and applies
> ointment and gauze to the inside of her
> cheek.)*

> *(She stuffs her things back into her bag.)*

**EMMIE.**  *(Pointing to the stained sweatshirt.)* What do I do
with that? Should I offer to pay for it? Do you know
how much they cost?

> *(**WENDY** comes banging in through the
> swinging doors. She waves a sweatshirt over
> her head.)*

**WENDY.** Who's tagging these??

**LOGAN.** Don't look at me?

**WENDY.** *(To* **EMMIE,** *wagging the sweatshirt in her face.)* Is it you, honey? Did you do this?

**EMMIE.** Did I do what? Is it wrong?

**LOGAN.** I tried to tell her. I didn't think she was doing it right.

**WENDY.** You mixed the serial number with the stock number!

**EMMIE.** *(To* **LOGAN.***)* You didn't try to tell me.

**WENDY.** I'm gonna be busting heads all day! These stupid things are ringing up at sixty-seven dollars a pop!

**LOGAN.** I asked if you were doing it right and you started talking about Blues Traveler.

**WENDY.** Sixty-seven! And then I have to go in and manually change each number.

**EMMIE.** I'm really sorry, I didn't realize it wasn't –

**WENDY.** And honey, the lines are long, Christmas is here.

**LOGAN.** I like your t-shirt, Wendy.

**WENDY.** I got it for $4.99, thank you very much.

**EMMIE.** I'll switch them. Can I go back in and switch them?

**LOGAN.** It might be too late for that.

**WENDY.** You can't be willy-nilly with the details.

**LOGAN.** Otis trained her.

**WENDY.** Otis trained you?

**EMMIE.** I'll fix it all.

**WENDY.** What happened to your face?

LOGAN.  She already went to the doctor.

WENDY.  *(Noticing the bloody sweatshirt.)* And what happened to this shirt?

LOGAN.  Her face.

EMMIE.  But I can fix it.

WENDY.  How you gonna fix it, honey? Blood doesn't come out unless you hit it with cold water and this one here just looks smeared and stained.

EMMIE.  Can I pay for it? Will I get fired?

WENDY.  Is this your first day?

EMMIE.  It's my fourth day.

LOGAN.  I'll talk to Otis. Let me talk to Otis.

EMMIE.  Don't talk to Otis, I just want to know how much the sweatshirt will cost to replace and if I don't have enough cash to cover it today, do you think Gar could maybe deduct it from my paycheck and then it'll be okay?

> *(GAR enters through the swinging doors.)*

GAR.  And then what will be okay?

> *(WENDY grabs the bloody sweatshirt from EMMIE.)*

WENDY.  Nothing! Nothing will be okay because these shirts are bloody!

GAR.  What?

WENDY.  That's why I'm back here. I keep finding all this flipping merchandise that's stained!

> *(GAR takes the sweatshirt from WENDY and examines it.)*

LOGAN.  There might be a problem with the manufacturer.

**WENDY.** I think the whole order came in soiled!

**LOGAN.** You should get on that, Gar.

**WENDY.** The customers are complaining!

**GAR.** Where are they?

**WENDY.** The customers?

**GAR.** The other sweatshirts that you found. The ones with the stains.

**WENDY.** I threw them away. *(Off* **GAR***'s look.)* What?

**GAR.** Wendy, what's the protocol for damaged merchandise?

**WENDY.** Gar, I didn't have time to find a manager, I was in the middle of what could have been a biohazardous calamity! Hello, I was a nurse for thirty-seven years, I knew to put those bad boys in a bag and toss them right in the dumpster!

**GAR.** Well go get them. They need to go back.

**WENDY.** I can't get them!

**GAR.** Why not?

**WENDY.** Because I –

**LOGAN.** Because I burned them.

> *(A moment.)*

**WENDY.** With fire.

> *(A moment.)*

That's the best way to handle toxic waste.

**LOGAN.** We've got your back Gar. We've got you.

> *(A moment.)*

**GAR.** Emmie, is this true?

EMMIE.  Huh?

GAR.  You've been tagging these all morning and you didn't notice anything?

LOGAN.  Sometimes a few bad ones just slip through. That's happened to me, too.

GAR.  Logan. Shut up.

> (*To* EMMIE.) Is that what happened?

> (*A moment.*)

EMMIE.  Yes.

> Yes.

> (*A moment.*)

> (**GAR** *looks at the three of them.*)

GAR.  Okay.

> Okay.

> Wendy, box up everything left from that order. We'll send it back.

WENDY.  Right-o.

GAR.  Logan?

LOGAN.  Yup?

GAR.  Never mind.

> Emmie?

> Emmie?

EMMIE.  Yes?

GAR.  Delete those scan numbers from the system.

> Do you know how to do that?

EMMIE.  Otis showed me.

**WENDY.** I can show her.

**GAR.** Well do it fast.

I have a training out in Rutland this afternoon and I want it done before I leave.

(**GAR** *starts to exit. He spots Emmie's belongings.*)

Personal items aren't allowed on the floor.

**WENDY.** She's not on the floor, she's in the warehouse.

**GAR.** *(To* **WENDY.***)* Mind your business, Wendy.

*(To* **EMMIE.***)* It's page four of the Employee Handbook.

**EMMIE.** I – I'm sorry, Otis said there weren't any lockers left and I have to carry my belongings with me until one opens up and Berry's isn't responsible if my things get stolen.

**GAR.** Not my problem. Until one is ready, you cannot have personal items with you.

**LOGAN.** But Otis said –

**GAR.** I'm not talking to Otis, I'm talking to her. And if you keep running your mouth, I'll be talking to you next. Got it?

I'm sorry – I didn't catch that.

Do you understand?

**LOGAN.** Yes, Gar.

I understand.

**GAR.** Thank you. *(To* **EMMIE.***)* Stealing is a federal offense. I'll turn you right over to the police and you'll be prosecuted to the fullest extent of the law if I catch you kidnapping our goods.

**EMMIE.** I wasn't kidnapping.

**GAR.** Put these things in your car during your next break.

**EMMIE.** Okay.

**GAR.** If you go one minute over, I'll dock you and write you up for time theft.

Do you understand?

**EMMIE.** Yes.

> *(He stares at her.)*

I understand.

**GAR.** Not the best way to get your first week started.

And take that Walkman off.

> *(****GAR**** *exits through the swinging doors.)*

> *(A moment.)*

**LOGAN.** Time theft?

**WENDY.** I need a drink and it's not even noon.

**LOGAN.** *(Imitating* **GAR.***)* "Do you understand?"

He's such a fucking hypocrite.

**WENDY.** The holidays are stressful for everyone.

**LOGAN.** He'll be more stressed if I start talking to folks.

**WENDY.** Alright, alright.

**LOGAN.** Emmie, ask Gar what's in the white boxes in aisles ten, twelve and fourteen.

**WENDY.** Take it easy.

**EMMIE.** *(Putting her Walkman in her backpack.)* I've never been yelled at like that before at work.

**LOGAN.** Welcome to Berry's.

**WENDY.** Oh honey, I get yelled at all the time.

**LOGAN.** No she doesn't.

**WENDY.** I do!

**LOGAN.** You're always coming up with shit to stay out of trouble.

**WENDY.** *(To* **EMMIE.***)* My husband's a traffic cop. I know how to keep cool under pressure.

**EMMIE.** What if I didn't have a car?

**LOGAN.** What?

**EMMIE.** If I didn't have a car where would I keep my coat and stuff?

**LOGAN.** You find little hiding spots.

**WENDY.** Maxine keeps losing her locker privileges and last week she was hiding her purse in the dairy fridge.

*(A moment.)*

**LOGAN.** Don't cry.

**EMMIE.** I'm not.

**LOGAN.** Don't cry.

You hear me? Either quit or suck it up and deal with it.

You broke your face? You can't pay rent? You need this job?

**EMMIE.** Yes.

**LOGAN.** Then you're just like the rest of us. So don't fucking cry.

**WENDY.** Oh, be quiet. She's nervous, not stupid.

*(***WENDY*** pats ***EMMIE*** on the arm.)*

It'll get better, honey.

**LOGAN.** No it won't.

WENDY.  *(Looking at* EMMIE*'s hands.)* Oh, you gotta get a good lotion.

EMMIE.  I use lotion every day.

WENDY.  Well then you need a pair of gloves. You're going to get all these little cuts from the boxes.

LOGAN.  And don't forget about my show! Okay? I'll get you a flyer! It's on the twenty-eighth.

WENDY.  *(To* LOGAN *as they start to exit.)* I'm going to finish my shift, have three nice drinks and take myself to bed. One nice, two nice, three nice.

LOGAN.  You better drink at home! The storm's a-coming!

WENDY.  But I love drunk driving in the snow.

>       (LOGAN *and* WENDY *exit through the swinging doors.)*
>
>       (EMMIE *begins de-tagging and de-scanning.)*
>
>       *(The holiday music* continues to play.)*

---

* Please refer to note on page 13.

## Three

*(The next day. The breakroom. Early evening. Different holiday music\*.)*

*(**MAXINE** comes into the breakroom. She stands on the table and pushes up one of the ceiling tiles. She pulls her purse and coat from a hiding spot in the vents.)*

*(**EMMIE** enters and tries to punch out on the time clock. She keeps getting an angry error beep each time she dips her card.)*

*(**MAXINE** hops off the table and puts her coat on over her employee vest. She checks her pager.)*

**MAXINE.** *(To her beeper.)* Fuck. Fuck you.

*(**EMMIE** looks at her.)*

Not you.

Are you done?

**EMMIE.** Hi. Yeah, almost.

*(She tries her card again. Beep!)*

**MAXINE.** I have to pick up my kids.

**EMMIE.** Sorry.

*(She tries once more. Beep!)*

**MAXINE.** I gotta get my paycheck.

**EMMIE.** Okay.

---

\* A license to produce *Paris* does not include a performance license for any third-party or copyrighted music. Licensees should create an original composition or use music in the public domain. For further information, please see the Music and Third Party Materials Use Note on page iii.

**MAXINE.** What'd you do? Break it?

**EMMIE.** It wasn't working when I came in.

**MAXINE.** This place is a piece of fucking shit, I swear to
God.

> (*She leans down and unplugs the time clock.*)

> (**WENDY** *enters.*)

**WENDY.** Max, go get your check! They're finally ready.

**MAXINE.** I'm trying.

**WENDY.** They were a day late coming in and Otis didn't
even apologize!

> (*She spots a plate of homemade Christmas
> cookies on the table.*)

Oh yum!

Who made the cookies?

> (**MAXINE** *plugs the timeclock back in. It beeps
> back to life.*)

**MAXINE.** Peggy. They taste like assholes.

> (*She takes Emmie's card and punches it.
> Success.*)

**EMMIE.** Oh wow, thank you.

> (**MAXINE** *grabs her own card and punches it.*)

**MAXINE.** I told you, I gotta get my kids, I didn't do it for
you.

> (**MAXINE** *exits.*)

**WENDY.** Her children are very bad people. If they were
yours, you'd be miserable too. And there are four of
them.

**EMMIE.** I heard.

**WENDY.** I shouldn't say such non-Christian stuff.

**EMMIE.** It's okay.

**WENDY.** And on Christmas Eve!

**EMMIE.** It's not Christmas Eve yet. You're in the clear.

**WENDY.** It's not?

**EMMIE.** It's only the 23$^{rd}$.

**WENDY.** Goddamn. My brain is jelly.

This time of year, I'll tell you what.

**EMMIE.** I know. All the days start to blur together.

> (**WENDY** *sits at the table. She is happy to be off her feet.*)

**WENDY.** Ah, my god. Finally.

**EMMIE.** Will the smell of eggs bother you?

**WENDY.** No honey. Eat.

> (**EMMIE** *sits at the table and unpacks a little snack. She unwraps hardboiled eggs from tinfoil.*)

> (**WENDY** *takes a flask from her purse and drinks. She rummages through her bag and takes four Ibuprofen. She washes them down with whatever is in her flask.*)

> (*She offers it to* **EMMIE.**)

**EMMIE.** No thank you.

**WENDY.** You don't drink?

**EMMIE.** I do, I just have to work later tonight and –

*(GAR enters. He is wearing a Christmas sweater and whistling a happy tune.)*

**GAR.** Hello, lovely ladies! Miss Emmie.

And Wendy Bendy, how's it going?

**WENDY.** Just great, honey. Life's a peach.

*(Still whistling, he grabs his belongings from a locker.)*

**GAR.** Favorite Rolling Stones song! Go!

**WENDY.** "I Will Survive."

**GAR.** Wendy. That's not the Stones.

**WENDY.** Oh darn. I lose.

**GAR.** And no, Emmie, no eating in the breakroom!

**EMMIE.** Oh! I thought we could –

**GAR.** Just kidding, just kidding, relax. This place is your home, I told you that!

**WENDY.** Someone's in a good mood.

**GAR.** Ask me why.

**WENDY.** Why?

**GAR.** I'm not telling!

**WENDY.** *(To EMMIE.)* Ask him why he's in a good mood.

**EMMIE.** Why are you in a good mood?

*(He pulls out a scratch off ticket and sticks it in WENDY's face.)*

**GAR.** Bam!

**WENDY.** Woo-hoo! Congratulations!

**GAR.** That's what I'm talking about!

**WENDY.** How much did you win?

*(He whispers something in her ear.)*

Get out of here!

**GAR.** I know!

**WENDY.** Well, no wonder you're so happy.

**GAR.** Now I can get in on the poker game tonight –

*(He does a little dance to celebrate poker.)*

**WENDY.** Ah, you're going to steal Greg and Sandy's money.

**GAR.** I'm going to *earn* Greg and Sandy's money and then I'm going to drink beer –

**WENDY.** What kind of beer?

**GAR.** Ottawa Blue.

**WENDY.** I thought you were watching your calories.

**GAR.** Ottawa Blue Light.

**WENDY.** I miss playing poker.

**GAR.** And then I'm going to sing karaoke for the masses. What's my specialty, you ask? Disney princess ballads.

**WENDY.** Alright. Well. You be careful on the roads. End of the month.

**GAR.** No one's going to ticket me for drunk driving! I'm too happy! Life is too good.

*(To* **EMMIE.***)* Maybe I'll see you at work? Do a duet?

**EMMIE.** Maybe.

*(He punches out on the timeclock, humming show tunes, salutes them, and exits.)*

**WENDY.** You work at Blonde Jovi??

**EMMIE.** Yeah. My shift starts at seven.

**WENDY.** I've never seen you there!

**EMMIE.** I'm just a waitress. And I –

> *(She chokes on a little piece of egg and coughs.)*

I – only started back in May.

> *(She keeps coughing.* **WENDY** *gets a cup of water from the water cooler.)*

**WENDY.** How old are you?

**EMMIE.** Twenty-two.

**WENDY.** You got kids?

**EMMIE.** *(Coughing.)* No.

**WENDY.** Drink that.

> **(EMMIE** *drinks and wipes the coughing tears from her face.)*

**EMMIE.** Just went down – wrong pipe, I think.

Thank you – sorry.

> **(WENDY** *sips from her flask.)*

> **(EMMIE** *eats her eggs.)*

Would you like an egg?

**WENDY.** No, sweetie, thank you. I'm waiting for my stupid husband to pick me up so we can go to a stupid holiday party at his stupid sister's house.

**EMMIE.** That sounds nice.

> *(A moment.)*

Gar seemed like he was in a good mood.

**WENDY.** Don't trust it. You hear me?

**EMMIE.** Okay.

**WENDY.** He used to pull that shit when he was on the floor with us.

One minute he's happy as a mental patient, the next he's ready to kick eight shades of shit out of you. And now that he's King Banana? Don't trust it. Just do your work and double check your pay stubs.

**EMMIE.** Okay.

Thank you.

**WENDY.** Did he touch you?

**EMMIE.** What? No, no, he's fine. I just –

I'm not sure he likes me. Sometimes he's nice, sometimes he's not so nice.

**WENDY.** It's like dating.

**EMMIE.** But is it crazy that I want him to like me? Is that stupid?

**WENDY.** No no, it's not stupid. We're all like that with the bosses a little bit.

**EMMIE.** Maybe I'm just tired.

*(A moment.)*

**WENDY.** Well. He should be nicer to you, I agree.

**EMMIE.** I'm not saying that. He's just doing his job.

**WENDY.** Yeah, no, I know, but –

You two have – stuff in common.

**EMMIE.** I guess.

**WENDY.** Not that you need advice from me. You work down at that Viking bar. You know how to deal with creeps.

**EMMIE.** We get a lot of them.

**WENDY.**  And you're pretty too. I wasn't cute enough to bartend. And I have no patience. Drunk guys in my face? 1-800-GO-AWAY.

**EMMIE.**  But you're so nice.

**WENDY.**  I'm not nice. I'm old.

**EMMIE.**  You helped me the other day.

**WENDY.**  Yeah. Well. That's how we do.

Your face feeling any better?

**EMMIE.**  Little by little.

**WENDY.**  Someone do that to you?

**EMMIE.**  No. I fell.

**WENDY.**  It's not my business.

**EMMIE.**  No, I really fell right after Thanksgiving. I was drunk at work and slipped in the parking lot. The ice –

**WENDY.**  Yeah. You look like a hockey player.

You have health insurance?

**EMMIE.**  No. And I missed two weeks of shifts.

**WENDY.**  *(Wincing.)* Yikes.

**EMMIE.**  So.

**WENDY.**  Yeah. They'll get you.

It's very stressful.

**EMMIE.**  It might've been a good thing, though. I was going to drive home that night.

**WENDY.**  No, you don't want that. You're too young to starting racking up DWIs.

**EMMIE.**  I can't lose my car.

**WENDY.**  No, you can't. I told my son that and he didn't listen.

*(A moment.)*

You know even these jerks at Berry's will let us use the parking lot to sleep in our cars if we're between places. Are you worried about being between places?

**EMMIE.**  No. I'll be okay. I'll get paid soon.

**WENDY.**  You'll be in the next cycle. You'll get your paycheck.

Who's your landlord, who are you renting from?

**EMMIE.**  The Sunshine Company.

**WENDY.**  Ugh! They're just the –

**EMMIE.**  I fell behind a month one time –

**WENDY.**  That's nothing!

**EMMIE.**  – and they sent the guy to unscrew my front door. He took it away until I came up with the balance. You could see right into my apartment.

**WENDY.**  Oh Jesus, I swear.

Everybody's just boiling up from the inside.

*(A moment.)*

What are you doing for the holidays?

**EMMIE.**  I'm not too sure. Tomorrow I work a double. Christmas Day –

**WENDY.**  You don't spend it with your family?

**EMMIE.**  My father lives in Hartford.

**WENDY.**  What about your mom?

I'm sorry, I'm being nosy.

**EMMIE.**  It's okay. She died a few years ago.

**WENDY.**  Oh shit, isn't that the worst? My mother died sixteen years ago and I think about her every day.

**EMMIE.** Yeah. Me too.

**WENDY.** She had a stroke and couldn't talk anymore. I think that's what really killed her. She was even more chatty than me.

**EMMIE.** Yeah. My mom got sick too.

**WENDY.** Oh honey.

**EMMIE.** I was down in DC and I –

I had to come back home to help.

**WENDY.** You're from Paris?

**EMMIE.** I am.

**WENDY.** What were you doing in DC?

I'm sorry, I'm being nosy.

**EMMIE.** I was going to college down there.

**WENDY.** Oh wow.

You gonna go back? You gotta go back.

**EMMIE.** Yeah, I want to. I have to figure out some money stuff first but –

Yeah.

*(A moment.)*

**WENDY.** Well, don't get stuck.

I tell my son that all the time.

Don't get stuck.

**EMMIE.** I won't.

**WENDY.** You got a boyfriend?

**EMMIE.** No.

**WENDY.** A girlfriend?

**EMMIE.** I'm single.

WENDY.  Well, you won't be for long. You're cute as a button.

Gotta get a nice someone to give you gifts, make you eggnog, rub your feet on Christmas.

> (WENDY *passes the flask to* EMMIE. EMMIE *takes a long sip.*)

EMMIE.  It's minty.

WENDY.  It's 100 proof. That mint will take your head right off.

> (EMMIE *takes another sip.*)

> (MAXINE *comes back into the breakroom. She's got her paycheck in hand.*)

MAXINE.  Where's Gar?

WENDY.  He just left.

MAXINE.  Fuck.

WENDY.  You might be able to catch him. He's going to poker at Sandy's.

MAXINE.  Oh good, he's playing cards while I'm missing money. Two frigging days before Christmas. Gimme that thing.

> (She takes the flask from WENDY.)

WENDY.  What happened?

MAXINE.  (*Showing* WENDY *her paycheck.*) This shit. Again. Where they keep –

WENDY.  Ugh. That was me last month. They don't care. (*To* EMMIE.) Double check your hours.

MAXINE.  What am I supposed to do? It's like a hundred and twenty bucks short.

WENDY.  Otis is coming in for night managing –

**MAXINE.** What time is he in?

**WENDY.** Not 'til seven.

**MAXINE.** So I'm paying a babysitter this whole time because of a mistake *they* made and you think they're going to reimburse me for the hour of childcare?

**WENDY.** You want to borrow the money you're missing from me?

**MAXINE.** No, I don't want to borrow the money from you, Wendy.

**WENDY.** Well then ask Otis.

**MAXINE.** Otis isn't going to give me anything.

Nobody's going to give me anything.

(*A moment.*)

**EMMIE.** Wendy and I were just talking about that. How stressful things are this time of year.

**MAXINE.** Oh, were you now?

**EMMIE.** Yeah. I'm sorry that happened with your check. I know what that's like.

**MAXINE.** Do you?

You know what it's like to have four kids? You know what it's like to live in one room?

**WENDY.** Max, stop it.

**MAXINE.** No, she's saying she knows things are stressful and I'm just curious what she has to be stressed about.

**WENDY.** She has a dead mother. That's very stressful.

**MAXINE.** (*To* **EMMIE.**) Who are you again?

I don't even know your name.

**EMMIE.** I'm Emmie. I'm new.

**MAXINE.** Okay, New Emmie –

**WENDY.** She's trying to be nice.

**MAXINE.** I don't need nice. I need my money.

**WENDY.** *(Handing* **MAXINE** *the tin of Christmas cookies.)* Okay okay, have a crappy cookie, take it easy.

> *(***DEV** *enters.)*

**DEV.** Yeah, Max, take it easy.

**WENDY.** *(Giving him a kiss.)* You just snuck in here.

**DEV.** What's wrong tonight, Maxine? Someone cut you in line at the post office? You didn't get enough champagne in your mimosa?

**WENDY.** / Stop, she's upset.

**MAXINE.** Fuck you, Dev.

**DEV.** Awww, no respect for the uniform?

**MAXINE.** I didn't think the town gave traffic cops real uniforms.

**WENDY.** You two, stop it. *(To* **DEV.***)* Honey, do you know Emmie? She works at Blonde Jovi!

**DEV.** *(Shaking* **EMMIE***'s hand.)* Hello hello hello, nice to meet you, Emily.

**WENDY.** Emmie.

**DEV.** Have we met?

**EMMIE.** You were here during my interview.

**DEV.** Oh, that's right. How could I forget?

**WENDY.** He never forgets a face.

**DEV.** And she's very noticeable.

**MAXINE.** You're an idiot.

**DEV.** *(To* **EMMIE.***)* You never called me!

**EMMIE.** Well I got hired here and I have my other job at the bar.

**DEV.** You like working for Mike?

**EMMIE.** He's great. He hired me even though I had never cocktail waitressed before.

**DEV.** Well, he's smart. Went to jail for like fifteen years, I think he picked up a thing or two.

**WENDY.** He could be smarter. He still makes all the girls wear skirts, right?

**EMMIE.** Yeah, if you're on the floor, you can't wear pants.

**WENDY.** It's like Hooters.

**DEV.** Well, that's how they make the money. Don't razz it. *(To EMMIE.)* You make good tips over there, right?

**EMMIE.** They're okay, not great. Especially during winter.

**DEV.** What do you girls pull a night?

**WENDY.** Mr. Nosy, can you mind your own business please? / Thank you very much.

**DEV.** No, I'm just curious. Sometimes I think these kids make more than we do.

**MAXINE.** They should, they probably work more / than you do.

**DEV.** *(To EMMIE.)* Like what? Like seventy, seventy-five bucks a night?

Or for you, probably a cool even hundred. Right? Am I right?

**MAXINE.** You better not be making a hundred fucking dollars a night.

**DEV.** I know these guys. They tip a little more for – different flavor.

**MAXINE.** I applied to work there twice and Mike wouldn't hire me. What do you have that I don't?

DEV. She's got a good personality, Max. Most people don't like to be cursed at all the time.

MAXINE. When's your birthday?

EMMIE. I'm a Libra.

MAXINE. People pleasers.

(To DEV.) And stop getting cute. I hope she does make more money than you do giving out parking tickets at the mall.

EMMIE. I'm not making a hundred dollars a night.

DEV. I think it's actually the speeding tickets that get me the extra dough.

MAXINE. I was going fifty.

DEV. You were doing seventy. In a school zone.

WENDY. Okay okay okay okay, let's go. / Your sister's olive loaf is waiting.

DEV. Wendy, hand on a sec.

(To EMMIE.) You don't want to say? That's okay, I know, I know the tricks.

EMMIE. I'm not playing a trick.

DEV. Mikey's always telling me bartenders don't like to say how much they make because then people get cheap and don't want to tip. It's good psychology, I gotta respect that.

EMMIE. No one likes to say how much they make.

MAXINE. Thank you, especially if / it isn't shit.

DEV. But see? That's not true. Wealthy people? They talk about money all the time. That's how they get wealthy.

MAXINE. No, they don't.

EMMIE. Not in my experience.

**DEV.** It's how they break the slave mentality.

**MAXINE.** / Oh my god, shut up!

**WENDY.** Alright, Dev, enough.

**DEV.** No no no no, not slave like that – *(To* **EMMIE.***)* no offense – I meant, mental slavery. Money slavery –

**MAXINE.** / Stop talking.

**DEV.** Rich people are rich because –

**MAXINE.** How many rich people do you know? They never talk about money!

**EMMIE.** They really don't.

It makes them feel guilty and uncomfortable.

**MAXINE.** When I worked for those fucking assholes down in Windsor Gardens, they would confess to being molested before they would say what they had in savings.

**EMMIE.** When I was in college –

**MAXINE.** This bitch went to college?

**EMMIE.** Just for a year and most of those kids wouldn't even say if their parents gave them money.

**MAXINE.** Thank you!

**DEV.** Okay, okay, but see, this is my point. Jason Juno says –

**WENDY.** / Please don't start.

**MAXINE.** Not this shit again.

**DEV.** *(To* **EMMIE.***)* I told you about Jason Juno, right? *Five Mini-Moves to Mega Millions*?

Okay, well he says we need more transparency about money. Pull it out in the open, talk about it with friends –

**MAXINE.** I talk about money all the time.

**DEV.** – and I think that's why rich people are rich. Because they don't shy away from it. They look money in the face and say, "Come to me!"

**WENDY.** Is that all / it takes?

**MAXINE.** Rich people are rich because they have rich fucking parents!

**DEV.** Well, what about the ones who don't? Huh? Huh? What about the self-made millionaires?

See? No answers.

That could be you!

That could be me! I'm breaking my chains and I'm ready to say, "Money! Over here!"

**MAXINE.** What chains are you breaking? You retired from one shitty job, couldn't afford to live on a fixed income, so your old ass got another shitty job that pays less. Freedom. Yay.

**DEV.** For now. For now. But Jason Juno has me taking responsibility for myself, my finances. Listen to me, Max, this is why you might be stuck. You're waiting for the world to give you something you should be giving yourself.

**MAXINE.** I'm sorry, should I be giving insurance to myself? Is that how the magical thinking works?

I'm stuck, you dumb bastard, because they won't pay me enough to live on.

**DEV.** You want more money? Make more money!

**MAXINE.** I'm trying to make more money, but my fucking bosses won't even pay me what they owe me as it is! *(She shoves her paycheck envelope into* **DEV***'s hands.)* Look at this. They keep screwing up our hours and no one cares! No one cares!

**DEV.**  Ah fuck, I'm sorry.

**MAXINE.**  How am I going to get stupid toys for Christmas?

That Taco Truck video game costs like –

**DEV.**  Yeah, yeah, no, that sucks.

**WENDY.**  Check Pick-a-Dollar. I'll check it tomorrow for you. They always have –

**MAXINE.**  They don't have what I need.

They don't have what I need.

*(A moment.)*

**DEV.**  You know what you really need?

You need to buy one of my Jason Juno books, because you'll learn that "even if life's mistakes don't fade, there is still money to be made!"

**WENDY.**  And on that note, we really are leaving.

**MAXINE.**  Divorce him, Wendy! Immediately! Please!

**WENDY.**  Wait for Otis and if he can't help out, call me.

**MAXINE.**  I'm not calling you, I'm going to rob Mr. Money Bags over here who just *thinks* money into existence.

**DEV.**  / Keep laughing.

**WENDY.**  Emmie, have a good shift tonight.

**EMMIE.**  Thank you. Have fun at the party.

**WENDY.**  / I won't.

**DEV.**  Oh, we definitely won't. Nice to meet you, honey. *(Winking.)* Keep an eye out for me at the bar.

**MAXINE.**  Yeah, he'll be trying to bum free drinks with all his millions.

**DEV.**  / That's how rich people stay rich.

WENDY. *(To* MAXINE *and* DEV.*)* You two, make up. No fighting on Christmas. *(To* EMMIE.*)* They do this once a week.

DEV. *(Hugging* MAXINE.*)* Come on, Max. Home is where the hug is.

> *(*WENDY *goes over to* MAXINE, *kisses her goodbye and gives her the flask.)*

WENDY. Keep this. Bye, sweetie.

MAXINE. Bye.

WENDY. I hope you never die. I would be very sad.

EMMIE. Good night, Wendy.

> *(*WENDY *punches out on the timeclock.)*

WENDY. We will survive another day!

> *(*WENDY *and* DEV *exit.)*

> *(*EMMIE *finishes eating.* MAXINE *watches her.)*

MAXINE. Where are you from?

EMMIE. Paris.

MAXINE. Why don't I know you?

EMMIE. I don't know.

MAXINE. You don't know?

EMMIE. I don't know.

> *(A moment.)*

My first shift back I made twenty-three bucks.

MAXINE. I'd take twenty-three fucking bucks right now.

> *(A moment.)*

You got a cigarette?

**EMMIE.** No.

**MAXINE.** *(Sighing.)* I shouldn't smoke anyway. They give me headaches.

You got a car?

**EMMIE.** Yes.

Do you need a ride somewhere?

**MAXINE.** *(Imitating* **EMMIE.***)* No, I don't need a "ride somewhere." Fuck you.

Sorry.

*(A moment.)*

(**MAXINE** *drinks from her flask.)*

You know your rising sign?

**EMMIE.** No.

**MAXINE.** Yeah, most people don't.

(**EMMIE** *stands and starts putting on her coat, etc.)*

You seem like a Cancer rising to me. Do you know what time of day you were born?

**EMMIE.** I'd have to find my birth certificate.

**MAXINE.** Get it from your mother. Oh wait, shit, no. Get it from your father.

**EMMIE.** We don't speak.

**MAXINE.** You don't have an aunt or an uncle who knows when you were born?

**EMMIE.** No.

**MAXINE.** Well shit, now I don't feel so bad, your life fucking sucks too.

If you can find out where and when you were born, I have a number you can call to get your whole astrological chart.

It's free too, even though she's the real deal.

**EMMIE.** Thank you. That'd be nice.

*(A moment.)*

**MAXINE.** Okay. Well.

I don't work tomorrow. So.

**EMMIE.** So.

Merry Christmas?

**MAXINE.** Yeah. I guess.

**EMMIE.** Thanks. Bye.

I hope everything works out with Otis / and your paycheck.

**MAXINE.** Yeah yeah yeah. Get going. Merry Christmas.

*(**EMMIE** exits.)*

*(**MAXINE** finishes what's left in the flask.)*

## Four

*(The next day, Christmas Eve. In the warehouse. Different holiday music\* through the speakers.)*

*(CARLISLE is in the warehouse. He is looking for someone or something between the aisles and stacks. He examines the contents of the boxes. He wears a leather vest.)*

*(EMMIE comes into the warehouse through the swinging doors. She stops when she sees him.)*

**EMMIE.**  Hello.

**CARLISLE.**  Hello.

**EMMIE.**  Hi.

**CARLISLE.**  I'm looking for Gar.

**EMMIE.**  For who?

**CARLISLE.**  Is he here?

**EMMIE.**  I don't know.

No. He's not in today. Or if he is, I haven't seen him.

**CARLISLE.**  What's your name?

**EMMIE.**  Emmie. I'm new.

**CARLISLE.**  Emmie.

**EMMIE.**  Do you work here?

**CARLISLE.**  Do I look like I work here?

**EMMIE.**  No.

---

\* A license to produce *Paris* does not include a performance license for any third-party or copyrighted music. Licensees should create an original composition or use music in the public domain. For further information, please see the Music and Third Party Materials Use Note on page iii.

CARLISLE.  I used to work here. There used to be pictures of me on the walls behind where you're standing.

You've never seen them?

EMMIE.  I just started.

*(A moment.)*

CARLISLE.  She just started.

*(He looks at her.)*

Emmie.

Is that short for something?

EMMIE.  Emaani.

CARLISLE.  But that's a beautiful name. Emaani. Why you don't go by that?

EMMIE.  People always mispronounce it.

CARLISLE.  You're like Gar. His full name is really –

Shit, I can't pronounce it. But "Gar" is short for something else.

What's your last name?

EMMIE.  When did you work here?

CARLISLE.  Oh, she's smart.

I worked here a very very very long time ago. Back before this place was even a Berry's.

EMMIE.  When it was still King Koupon?

CARLISLE.  Yes! Back when it was King Koupon! How do you know about this?

EMMIE.  I remember from when I was young. We used to shop there.

CARLISLE.  You're from Paris?

EMMIE.  Yes.

**CARLISLE.** Ah, you don't look like it. I was thinking maybe New York City.

**EMMIE.** I'm not from New York.

**CARLISLE.** Who would want to be, right? Big, loud, dirty.

And the rents? Come on, Emmie. That's – it's a crime what they do down there.

**EMMIE.** The rents can be high here, too.

**CARLISLE.** No. Here? Little old Paris?

**EMMIE.** I pay two fifty.

**CARLISLE.** To live where?

**EMMIE.** I live –

*(A moment.)*

**CARLISLE.** Yeah.

She's smart.

*(He looks at her.)*

So no Gar today?

**EMMIE.** No. I don't think so.

**CARLISLE.** Because Gar usually works a lot of days.

Maybe today he's not feeling well. Maybe he's pulling a sickie, leaving you with all the work on Christmas Eve.

**EMMIE.** I'm not doing all the work.

**CARLISLE.** No? Are there other workers here with you? Helping like little elves?

**EMMIE.** Yes.

I mean, not back here right now, there aren't many, but on the – in the store. There are a lot of people out there.

**CARLISLE.** You want to be my little elf?

Come work for me in my Christmas shop?

(**EMMIE** *looks at him.*)

Gar – has he told you how he works for Santa?

**EMMIE.** J already have a job.

Two, actually. I have two jobs.

**CARLISLE.** What's your other job?

**EMMIE.** I –

**CARLISLE.** Go ahead.

**EMMIE.** I work at a bar.

**CARLISLE.** Oh well, come on, that's fun!

Party time!

That's a good job, right?

**EMMIE.** Sometimes, yeah.

**CARLISLE.** You're making tips, making drinks.

**EMMIE.** I don't make drinks, I just serve them.

**CARLISLE.** Yeah, but. You like to drink the drinks, right? Am I right?

Come on, don't lie.

**EMMIE.** I drink drinks, yes.

**CARLISLE.** What you like to drink? Beer? Little wine cooler?

**EMMIE.** I drink vodka.

**CARLISLE.** With coke? With seltzer?

**EMMIE.** On the rocks.

**CARLISLE.** Oh. Okay. She –

She wants to feel alive.

*(A moment.)*

So you have two jobs. One good, and then this one.

You have this job unpacking boxes and then packing boxes and unpacking and packing and unpacking and selling all of this shit that will end up in the landfill.

This is good work to you?

**EMMIE.** It's a job. I like the people.

**CARLISLE.** Yeah?

**EMMIE.** Yeah.

**CARLISLE.** But you make so little money –

**EMMIE.** I make five an hour.

**CARLISLE.** That's what a life is worth to you?

*(He stares at her.)*

You hear about this warehouse – the new place they built outside Saint Albans? They ship – I think it's cordless phones around the country.

Yes? Am I making sense? Have you heard of this place?

**EMMIE.** No.

**CARLISLE.** Well, there was a woman who was working one afternoon, packing up phones on a hot day and she faints from the heat, hits her head and dies.

She dies on the floor.

And the bosses put cones around her body and tell everyone else to get back to work.

**EMMIE.** They don't do that here.

**CARLISLE.** Yet.

They don't do that here *yet.*

But just you wait – everyone everywhere is going to keep shopping just so they can feel safe at Christmastime and you will be dead on the floor.

(**EMMIE** *stares at him.*)

Your people are good workers. You'd be a good worker for me, I can tell.

**EMMIE.** I already have a job.

**CARLISLE.** Gar used to be good worker for me. But now I'm getting a little impatient.

Did he tell you what he does for me?

**EMMIE.** Gar doesn't tell me anything.

**CARLISLE.** He should. Because if you work for me, my job you can do while you're right here at this job. While you're opening your little boxes and making little notes.

Right? That sounds good, right? Making money on top of money?

It could probably help with this –

(*He reaches toward her bruised cheek.*)

Oh come on. I'm going to hurt you?

Stop.

(*He moves closer to her.*)

Broken teeth, right?

**EMMIE.** I fell.

**CARLISLE.** Vodka on the rocks.

Open up. Let's look.

(*A moment.*)

(*She opens her mouth.*)

Say aaaaaah.

*(She says "aaaaaah.")*

*(He places his hand on her face.)*

*(He peers into her mouth.)*

This damage? If she's working for me, she can pay this within two weeks.

EMMIE. Two weeks?

*(**LOGAN** comes into the warehouse.)*

*(**EMMIE** backs away from **CARLISLE**.)*

LOGAN. Hey, man.

CARLISLE. Hey. Man.

LOGAN. I told you –

CARLISLE. Yes?

LOGAN. Look, I told you he wasn't here.

CARLISLE. Yeah, but you told me without manners. So I didn't believe you.

LOGAN. It's what I said yesterday and the day before and the day before that.

CARLISLE. I wanted to look around for myself.

LOGAN. Cool. Why don't I just –

CARLISLE. Why don't you just what?

*(A moment.)*

You're a big guy now?

Tough guy.

Smart guy.

*(To* **EMMIE** *re:* **LOGAN***.)* This guy is smart too. All of you working at Berry's are so fucking smart. Maybe you can give some of these brains to your friend Gar and tell him he's two shipments late.

**LOGAN.** He's not my friend. And I don't give messages.

**CARLISLE.** *(To* **EMMIE***.)* But this one does.

You'll tell Gar that Mr. Carlisle stopped by to see him? And that if he doesn't come up with my two shipments, I'm going to visit his father in Grandview and give him a bath in boiling water?

You'll give him this message for me?

> *(***EMMIE** *looks at him.)*

**EMMIE.** Yes.

**CARLISLE.** Thank you. Thank you. And think on what I said before.

**EMMIE.** I will.

**CARLISLE.** *(To* **LOGAN***.)* Goodbye, smart guy. *(To* **EMMIE***.)* Goodbye, Emaani.

> *(***CARLISLE** *exits through the aisles of the warehouse.)*

**LOGAN.** Did I seem scared?

**EMMIE.** No, you seemed tough. I thought you were going to punch his lights out.

**LOGAN.** I would have! If it had come to that! I was writing new lyrics on my break, I'm fired up! You're coming to my show, right? It's Friday.

**EMMIE.** I was the scared one. I almost peed when he asked if I wanted to be his little elf.

**LOGAN.** Don't be his little anything.

**EMMIE.** Gar's dad is at Grandview?

**LOGAN.**  He has Alzheimer's.

**EMMIE.**  Oh.

>   *(A moment.)*

I lied.

**LOGAN.**  About what?

**EMMIE.**  I told that man Gar wasn't here even though he is.

**LOGAN.**  Relax. Look, Gar is just a dumb ass. Stay out of it.

**EMMIE.**  Stay out of what?

>   *(A moment.)*

**LOGAN.**  No.

**EMMIE.**  Tell me.

**LOGAN.**  There's nothing to tell.

**EMMIE.**  Tell me and I'll come to your show.

**LOGAN.**  How many tickets will you buy, evil woman?

**EMMIE.**  One.

**LOGAN.**  Not enough.

**EMMIE.**  Six.

>   *(A moment.)*

**LOGAN.**  Don't tell anyone.

**EMMIE.**  I won't.

**LOGAN.**  Don't tell anybody.

**EMMIE.**  I said I won't.

**LOGAN.**  Gar runs cigarettes for these weird guys.

**EMMIE.**  What does that mean?

**LOGAN.**  I don't know. I think he gets them cheap in Virginia and gets them shipped up here –

**EMMIE.** Like *here* here.

**LOGAN.** Yes – to Berry's – here. And then they sell them wherever for cheaper.

**EMMIE.** Is it legal?

**LOGAN.** Just don't tell anybody.

**EMMIE.** Why do you know?

**LOGAN.** I busted him one night unloading a shipment. He said if I didn't tell, he'd give me free cigarettes for a year.

> (**WENDY** *pokes her head through the swinging doors.*)

**WENDY.** Logan, you were supposed to do switchover with me.

**LOGAN.** Ah! Fuck. Yes. Okay, I'm coming.

**WENDY.** Too late.

**LOGAN.** I said I'm coming!

**WENDY.** Otis got Charmaine to do it.

**LOGAN.** Great. That's great!

**WENDY.** And he said he's taking you off the rotation.

**LOGAN.** Even better!

**WENDY.** That's thirty bucks a check, Logan.

**LOGAN.** Did you tell him I was working?

**WENDY.** I didn't know where you were.

**LOGAN.** Did you tell him I was covering for Gar's smuggling ass?

**WENDY.** No, I didn't tell him that. And you shouldn't be talking about it either.

**LOGAN.** Where's Otis? I need that fucking extra pay.

WENDY. Well, cursing isn't going to get you what you need.

LOGAN. Thanks, mom! I really appreciate the etiquette lesson!

WENDY. Hey, be nice. It's Christmas Eve.

LOGAN. I am nice! I'm a nice guy and I'm full of festive holiday fucking cheer but I'm tired and my feet fucking hurt and I had to lie to that weird fucking guy and I'm scared that no one is going to come to my fucking show and I don't need Otis taking money from my paycheck!

WENDY. Just talk to him.

LOGAN. I don't want to talk to him! I just want to complain! Is that okay, Wendy? Is it? Can I be tired of my minimum wage sadness for one fucking day even if it is Christmas Eve?

Yaaaaaaaah!

> *(He picks up a chair and throws it into the shelves. Boxes fly everywhere.)*

> *(A long moment.)*

> *(**GAR** comes into the warehouse.)*

> *(He sees **EMMIE**, **LOGAN**, and **WENDY** not working.)*

> *(He sees the downed boxes and nudges one with his foot. The sound of broken glass jingles from inside.)*

> *(Another long moment.)*

GAR. You know –

LOGAN. Gar –

GAR. – every time I come back here now, I see the three of you together.

**LOGAN.** Don't start with us, man.

**GAR.** *(Pointing in their faces.)* One. Two. Three.

Why is that?

Wendy?

**WENDY.** I don't know.

**GAR.** Oh, you can do better than that.

Spin us a fun story.

**WENDY.** I don't have a fun story.

**GAR.** Sure you do! Come on, I want to hear all about how you had to rush back here and tell these two that the boxes are covered in blood and let's burn them up with fire and destroy everything inside.

**WENDY.** I don't have a fun story. I came back here to get Logan for the switchover.

**LOGAN.** And I came back here to help Emmie.

**EMMIE.** And I was back here because a man named Carlisle said if he doesn't get his shipments, he's going to hurt your father at Grandview.

*(A long moment.)*

**GAR.** You're all fired.

| **EMMIE.** | **WENDY.** | **LOGAN.** |
|---|---|---|
| What?? Gar! | Are you nuts?? | Wait, what the fuck?! |

**GAR.** Gather your belongings, don't bother checking out, we'll send you your last paycheck in the mail.

**LOGAN.** You're going to fire us for trying to help?

**GAR.** You don't want to leave quietly? I'll call security.

**WENDY.** / Gar, don't do this.

**LOGAN.** And tell them what? What the fuck are you /
going to tell them?

**GAR.** I'll tell them the fucking truth, don't you curse at
me! That you three consistently steal time from Berry's,
that you come up with conspiracies / to cover up your
misdeeds, and that each one of you is in violation
of codes two, five and seven from the Employee
Handbook!

**LOGAN.** We've been trying to help you, and I wish we had
just handed you over to that psycho so he could feed
your ass to Champ.

**WENDY.** You two, stop it! We'll figure it out, no one needs
to fight like this before Christmas!

**LOGAN.** You're not going to tell anybody shit. Because you
know we'll all go right to corporate and tell them how
you've turned Berry's into your illegal fucking stash
house. *(Pointing to **EMMIE**.)* Her too! She knows, too,
we'll all fucking go.

**EMMIE.** I'm not going anywhere.

**WENDY.** We will do no such thing. Calm down! Both of
you!

*(A moment.)*

**GAR.** Prove it.

**WENDY.** Okay, enough. Emmie, go get Otis.

**GAR.** Please. Logan. Prove it. Enlighten me.

**LOGAN.** I don't want to do this, man. We're on the same
side.

**GAR.** Where is all this "stash" I'm hiding?

**LOGAN.** I know you make like three bucks more than we
do. I'm not trying to judge your side hustle, but you're
always pulling fucking rank.

*(**GAR** goes to a pile of crashed boxes.)*

**GAR.** Is it here? Is my "stash" hiding in one of these?

> *(He opens a box and dumps out the broken contents.)*

Oh no no no, that's just the merchandise you broke. Don't worry – we'll be sure to deduct that from your last paycheck.

**LOGAN.** Any chance you get, you pull out your three inches and piss all over everybody. / And I'm sick of it.

**GAR.** Don't you fucking threaten me! Don't you fucking look at me, / you white rapping piece of shit!

**WENDY.** Stop this! Both of you, stop this right now!

**GAR.** I'm going to get Otis.

**EMMIE.** Wait. Wait. Wait. Wait. Wait. Wait. Please.

Gar.

Please. This is – this is a misunderstanding. I didn't –

He won't – no one is going to say anything about anything to anyone.

Logan is just – he's nervous because of his show and I was back here and I talked to that guy but I don't –

We won't – we will stop being back here stealing company time.

Please.

**WENDY.** Gar. It's Christmas.

She's got bills to pay.

I can't fall behind again. I can't.

Please. Please.

> *(A long moment.)*

**GAR.** Okay. Alright.

> *(A wave of relief.)*

**WENDY.** Oh fucking shit. Thank you, Gar. Thank you very much.

**EMMIE.** We won't do anything – we won't do anything upsetting anymore.

> *(**GAR** looks at **LOGAN**.)*

> *(A moment.)*

**LOGAN.** Thank you.

**GAR.** You're welcome.

> *(A moment.)*

Someone has to pay for this damaged merchandise.

**LOGAN.** It's on me. I'll get it.

**GAR.** I'll tally up the total and / take it from your paycheck.

**LOGAN.** You'll take it from my paycheck.

Of course you will.

**GAR.** I want to make sure something like this doesn't happen again.

**EMMIE.** It won't.

**GAR.** Well, just to be safe – Logan, I'm putting you on overnight stocking Thursdays and Fridays through February.

> *(He starts to exit. **LOGAN** follows close behind him.)*

**LOGAN.** Hold up hold up hold up, I can't do Thursday. I have my show Thursday. I'm going to be in Burlington.

**GAR.** Not my problem.

**LOGAN.** Gar, please.

**GAR.** I'm sure you can find a way to work it out.

**LOGAN.** I'll do any other overnight. I'll do them through the summer. Just not this Thursday.

**GAR.** Thursday is when I need you.

**LOGAN.** This is our first show. I'm the lead MC, I have to be there. I don't know if you know how it works –

**GAR.** I know how rap music works, thank you very much.

If you can't do it, I'll find someone in the applicant pool who can.

**WENDY.** Gar –

**GAR.** *(A warning.)* Wendy.

*(To* **LOGAN.***)* You want to quit? No. You can't quit, you have your grandmother to think about.

**LOGAN.** But I – need this.

I need my show.

**GAR.** I'll see you Thursday.

> *(***LOGAN** *is devastated. He heads towards the doors and turns, his eyes full of sorrow.)*

> *(He exits.)*

> *(A moment.)*

**WENDY.** I need to go and –

I'm going to finish the switchover with Otis.

Merry Christmas.

> *(She leaves.)*

> *(***EMMIE** *and* **GAR** *in the warehouse.)*

*(A long moment.)*

(**EMMIE** *starts cleaning up the mess of boxes.*)

**GAR.**  Just leave it.

**EMMIE.**  I can help.

**GAR.**  Just –

Just leave it.

*(She stops cleaning.)*

What?

**EMMIE.**  Nothing.

**GAR.**  Then stop fucking looking at me.

Sorry.

Just – get back on the floor.

*(She stays where she is.)*

What?

*(A moment.)*

There's a bigger thing here that no one understands.

They don't get it – Logan thinks I'm heartless, but if I don't keep them in line –

What job do you have where you can just do whatever you want, be wherever you want, break whatever you want? I can't have employees running around, unaccounted for. There's a system here.

I'm fucking tired.

**EMMIE.**  Me too.

*(A moment.)*

**GAR.**  Did you get paid yet?

EMMIE. Not yet. Otis said my first check is on Friday.

GAR. What did Logan tell you?

EMMIE. About what?

GAR. About the stuff he / mentioned earlier.

EMMIE. Nothing. He didn't say nothing. / Anything.

GAR. Whatever. Forget it.

EMMIE. I could put in a good word for you at the bar. Mike hired me, he could hire you, too.

GAR. Thanks, but I'm good.

EMMIE. It's not a ton of money to start but –

GAR. No. No. No. What? No.

I just need –

*(A moment.)*

EMMIE. That man says – he said you're two shipments late.

GAR. That's because I've started selling to someone else.

EMMIE. Why?

GAR. Because fuck him.

*(A moment. He looks right at her.)*

Because I can see the future. And fuck him.

*(A moment.)*

GAR. I was wrong – clean this stuff up. I'll put a few extra hours on your paycheck.

EMMIE. I won't tell anybody. I won't say anything.

GAR. Okay. Okay. Sure. Great. Thanks. Bye.

Merry Christmas.

## Five

*(Five days later. Morning. Some of the Christmas decorations are still up, but most of the tree lights have blown out. The same plate of Christmas cookies sits on the table.)*

*(A "HAPPY NEW YEAR!" banner hangs above the door.)*

*(**EMMIE** and **MAXINE** sit at the table.)*

*(**MAXINE** is taking a quiz.)*

MAXINE. *(Reading.)* "True or False: I like to help people."

*(Reading.)* "True or False: I prefer small groups to large parties."

*(She makes a note on her page.)*

*(Reading.)* "Do you Mostly Agree, Sometimes Agree or Never Agree with the following statement: I wake up with a headache almost every day?"

Give me a break. What is this nonsense they have us doing? Did you take this one already?

EMMIE. I took mine yesterday. They said we had to to get paid.

MAXINE. Well they should have to pay us extra.

If I have to take an "End of the Year Opinion Survey," I want "End of the Year Opinion Money."

*(**LOGAN** comes in, sad as Eeyore, and punches in on the timeclock.)*

*(She takes her test.)*

What are these assholes going to be doing with my opinions anyway?

Logan, did you take one of these stupid tests?

(**LOGAN** *puts on his employee vest and grunts an indecipherable response.*)

Logan, sweetie, it's okay. There will be other shows.

(*He moans again and goes into the bathroom.*)

He's still taking it hard, huh?

**EMMIE.** It's almost been a week.

**MAXINE.** I wish I had that kind of time to be upset about shit that doesn't matter.

**EMMIE.** It matters to him.

**MAXINE.** I know, I know.

**EMMIE.** He's been looking forward to it.

**MAXINE.** Have you heard Logan rap?

**EMMIE.** Stop it.

**MAXINE.** Then you know that it's probably best for the Enemy Boyz that he wasn't there.

**EMMIE.** You're mean.

**MAXINE.** No I'm not.

**EMMIE.** Sometimes you are.

**MAXINE.** Whatever. Shut up. Fuck you.

(*A moment.*)

(**MAXINE** *goes back to her quiz.*)

I'm not mean.

I'm real.

**EMMIE.** Okay.

**MAXINE.** When does your shift start?

**EMMIE.** Soon.

**MAXINE.** Good.

> *(A moment.)*

> *(**MAXINE** takes her quiz.)*

I've been thinking about trying to get out of here, anyways.

Charmaine went up to the job fair at the Holiday Inn and says they're hiring at the school in the dining halls again.

But I don't know.

I don't know if I can do those rich kids all day long.

Maybe I'll wait for the summer, do boat tours. You ever do the tours?

**EMMIE.** No.

**MAXINE.** It's so fucking annoying having to talk to tourists all day long, but it's better than here.

Plus, the tips can be really good. I mean, probably not Blonde Jovi good, but I get by.

> *(She looks at **EMMIE**.)*

I'm just kidding. What's wrong with you?

**EMMIE.** Nothing.

**MAXINE.** *(Imitating her.)* "Nothing."

My mother calls me again this morning screaming about having to babysit and I'm like, "Bitch, shut up, I'm trying to get a better job, you had it so easy." They had it so easy before us, they don't even know. My mother worked in that button factory for twenty-nine years. She made friends, had health insurance, had *dental* insurance. Got one week paid vacation. Come on. What the hell do we have? Personality tests and those shitty cookies.

I'd body slam a nun for a factory job, my God.

*(WENDY enters with a few envelopes in hand.)*

**WENDY.** I have paychecks! / Who wants money?

**MAXINE.** Thank you.

*(WENDY hands MAXINE her paycheck.)*

**WENDY.** *(To EMMIE.)* Honey, I tried to sign yours out, but Otis said I wasn't authorized.

**EMMIE.** I'll get it after my break.

**MAXINE.** La di da.

*(She opens up her check and examines it.)*

Thank. Fucking. / God.

**WENDY.** It's all there?

**MAXINE.** It's all here.

*(She sighs.)*

Yeah. All this week and last week's mistake they fixed.

*(WENDY sits down and opens her paycheck.)*

**WENDY.** Oh great. They took your mistake and gave it to me.

**EMMIE.** What happened?

**WENDY.** They only paid me for thirty-two hours and I worked forty-one!

Oh boy.

**MAXINE.** Go find Gar and slap his face.

**WENDY.** I can't. He's not here today.

**MAXINE.** Well get Otis and ream his ass.

**WENDY.** No. Otis is cranky because he's on a double. He yelled at me when I asked for the checks and says he can't be bothered right now.

**MAXINE.** Who cares? We're all cranky, you still have to do your job.

**WENDY.** Just leave it, Max.

**MAXINE.** Let me finish this stupid ass test and then I'll go talk to that grumpy bastard.

Cranky.

Please.

If Otis can't handle doubles, Otis shouldn't do doubles.

**WENDY.** He has to, he's covering for Gar. It's the fourth day in a row he hasn't shown up to work.

**MAXINE.** Who?

**WENDY.** Gar. Apparently he hasn't been in since Christmas Eve.

**MAXINE.** Whatever.

*(She takes her test.)*

He's probably off relaxing and kissing under the mistletoe while you're going broke.

*(A moment.)*

**EMMIE.** Gar hasn't been here since Christmas Eve?

**WENDY.** I guess so. That's what Otis said.

**MAXINE.** He was here yesterday.

**EMMIE.** You saw him?

**MAXINE.** Yeah, he was. I remember that because –

Oh, wait, no. That wasn't him.

**WENDY.**  I gotta call Dev about my check.

**EMMIE.**  Did anyone call him?

**WENDY.**  Dev?

**EMMIE.**  No. Gar.

**WENDY.**  Dev and I were going to take the train to Montreal for New Year's on Sunday, but I don't think I can go now that my check is short.

Shoot.

**MAXINE.**  What's in Montreal?

**WENDY.**  We were going to dinner at the steak house we used to go to on Chevalier Street.

Is that how you pronounce it?

**MAXINE.**  Oh, I love that place. With the blue curtains behind the bar?

**WENDY.**  Yeah, isn't it nice?

**MAXINE.**  It's gorgeous.

**WENDY.**  I love their mashed potatoes. They put chives and a little bit of cheese in them.

But now I'm not sure we can go.

**MAXINE.**  No. Wendy. You have to go.

Call Dev.

See if Jason Juno has any suggestions for how to find cash in a pinch.

**WENDY.**  Yeah.

I'll call Dev.

*(A moment.)*

**EMMIE.**  Has he ever missed a day of work without calling in?

**WENDY.**  Who?

**EMMIE.**  Gar.

**WENDY.**  No.

I don't know, but I don't think so.

**MAXINE.**  Maybe he went away for the holidays.

**WENDY.**  No. Otis said he's been a no-show this whole week.

**MAXINE.**  Maybe he's dead.

Ooops. Did I say that?

**WENDY.**  Maxine.

**MAXINE.**  Sorry.

                *(She takes her test.)*

**WENDY.**  I'm sure he's fine.

**MAXINE.**  Or –

                *(**WENDY** and **EMMIE** look at her.)*

**WENDY.**  What is that face?

**EMMIE.**  Or what?

**MAXINE.**  Nothing.

Nothing. Nothing.

**WENDY.**  I gotta call Dev.

**EMMIE.**  *(To **MAXINE**.)* You're not worried?

**MAXINE.**  About Gar? No. He's not worried about me, so I'm not thinking about him.

**EMMIE.**  Should we say something to Otis?

**MAXINE.**  You going to tell Otis what Gar gets up to with his little friends in the warehouse?

You know what Otis will say? *(To* **WENDY**.*) You* know what Otis will say.

He'll say if Gar slept with dogs, he should expect fleas.

**EMMIE.** If you missed four days of work –

**MAXINE.** You know it'd be because I was home with a stupid sick kid.

Look, I hope he's out with the flu. Or God forbid, having to take care of some stuff with his father. If not?

Well.

Let's just say I find it very ironic that he's such a stickler about the rules and all the while he's Al Capone back in the warehouse.

**EMMIE.** Okay.

(**LOGAN** *re-enters.*)

**MAXINE.** *(Re:* **LOGAN**.*)* Why don't you ask him? He's been wanting to pour bleach in Gar's coffee for the last week.

**LOGAN.** Ask me what?

**EMMIE.** Gar didn't come to work today.

**LOGAN.** Good.

**EMMIE.** Or the last three days.

**LOGAN.** Alright.

**EMMIE.** Wendy is trying to make sure he's okay.

**WENDY.** So are you.

**EMMIE.** Yeah, I am, I just –

**LOGAN.** I don't care about Gar.

**EMMIE.** Okay.

**LOGAN.** So?

**EMMIE.** So?

**LOGAN.** So what?

**EMMIE.** I – I don't know. Maybe something happened. `

**MAXINE.** You're new. Right?

You've known Gar for what? Two weeks?

**EMMIE.** Forget it.

**MAXINE.** You know what his favorite thing to do was? Schedule me on those swing shifts that have no end time. I'd show up to work not knowing how many hours I'd be here, who does that to someone with four kids? I'd be begging them for a set schedule and every week, it was the same shit. And I can't totally blame him – Capricorn. That's a sign that can deny and withhold, but he would never relent, so God bless Gar and I hope he hasn't gotten mixed up in some tragedy, *(She crosses herself.)* but there was not that much generosity in that man's soul.

And if God forbid he is dead *(She crosses herself.)* I'm not giving him special treatment.

Dead people feel very entitled because they're not around to defend themselves, and I cannot abide.

**EMMIE.** Maybe stop saying dead.

**LOGAN.** No one's dead. Maxine reads too many romance novels.

**WENDY.** I'm sure he's fine.

He's probably just dealing with his dad.

**MAXINE.** Or he's been dealing with those guys, in which case he might be – *(She crosses herself.)*

**WENDY.** Don't say things like that.

**EMMIE.** He wasn't "dealing" with those guys, he was working.

**MAXINE.** Okay.

**EMMIE.** He provided a service, they paid him.

**MAXINE.** That's not work. That's free illegal money.

**LOGAN.** I'd do it.

**WENDY.** Yeah, I would do it too. / Probably.

**EMMIE.** We all would.

**MAXINE.** I wouldn't.

**EMMIE.** Well, maybe you don't need the money as badly.

**MAXINE.** Well, maybe you don't tell me what I do and don't fucking need. I got four kids. What does Gar have?

**EMMIE.** A sick father.

**WENDY.** He has a car, Maxine. You don't have a car or payments.

**MAXINE.** So I'm supposed to feel bad for him because he drives a car and has a father in a fancy living facility? My father died at Newton Memorial and he was perfectly fine.

**EMMIE.** But we're not talking about your father.

**MAXINE.** You're all fucking idiots.

*(She gathers her things, starts to leave and turns back.)*

You know what? I'm not feeling bad for people because they make dumb dumb choices.

**EMMIE.** No one's asking you to feel bad.

**MAXINE.** He could've had more money if he hadn't spent all his money. And then he wouldn't be in trouble.

**WENDY.** Maybe he's not in trouble! Maybe he won another scratch-off ticket and went to the Catskills!

**MAXINE.** What did he pull a week?

**EMMIE.** I don't know.

**MAXINE.** Logan.

**LOGAN.** What?

**MAXINE.** What was Gar making every week?

**LOGAN.** How would I know?

**MAXINE.** What do you take home?

**WENDY & LOGAN.** After taxes?

**MAXINE.** Yes.

**LOGAN.** $183.

**MAXINE.** Okay, and that's at what? $5.50 an hour?

**LOGAN.** I'm at $5.75 an hour.

**MAXINE.** Okay, fuck you.

So Gar was probably like maybe nine an hour?

Forty hour weeks?

Three-sixty before taxes, maybe like two-eighty-five after?

**EMMIE.** It doesn't matter.

**MAXINE.** Yes, it does. If he was responsible with that two hundred and eighty bucks –

**WENDY.** Two-eighty-five.

**MAXINE.** – two hundred and eighty-five bucks, he could pay his rent, get food and gas and still have money left over for his dad.

**WENDY.** But he liked playing poker.

**MAXINE.** Yes! Exactly! He liked playing poker, so –

**WENDY.** And beer. He liked to drink beer.

**MAXINE.** See where I'm going with this?

**EMMIE.** No.

**WENDY.** Although I think historically light beer is a little cheaper.

**MAXINE.** He didn't have to do this. Whatever he was doing, he didn't have to. And if he's caught up in something –

**EMMIE.** Okay.

**MAXINE.** What?

**EMMIE.** Okay.

You're right.

Okay.

**MAXINE.** Don't placate me.

**EMMIE.** I'm not.

But we're talking about two very different things right now, so –

Okay. Gar was irresponsible.

And lazy –

**MAXINE.** That's not what I said.

**EMMIE.** Whatever.

Okay.

*(A moment.)*

**LOGAN.** You win, Max.

You win.

*(She looks at them.)*

**MAXINE.** One day I'll be dead, you fucking morons, and you'll realize that I was right all along.

*(She exits.)*

*(A moment.)*

WENDY.  I have to call Dev. I think we have to change our New Year's plans.

*(She clocks in on the time clock and exits.)*

LOGAN.  What?

EMMIE.  Nothing.

LOGAN.  What?

EMMIE.  Nothing. Logan. Fuck. Nothing.

*(A moment.)*

LOGAN.  Okay.

EMMIE.  He gave me a job.

He made me two ID badges.

You know they wouldn't hire me at Price Chopper because they don't put black people on the registers?

LOGAN.  That's not true.

EMMIE.  Yes, it is.

LOGAN.  They didn't say that to you.

EMMIE.  How would you know what they said to me?

*(A moment.)*

Why is everyone acting like they don't care?

LOGAN.  Because I kind of don't!

Sorry!

He took away my fucking show, he makes everyone here miserable –

EMMIE.  So what? Shouldn't we still try to help him?

LOGAN.  So go help him! Why do you need me?

EMMIE.  Because I thought –

I thought – I thought that's what you do. I thought we were all in this together.

*(A long moment.)*

**LOGAN.** Look. It's the holidays and I hate myself. If Gar doesn't turn up by tomorrow, we'll – I don't know.

What? We go to the cops?

Is that what you want to do? Tell them what we know, what we heard, what that guy said?

**EMMIE.** Can we do that?

**LOGAN.** Sure.

Let's take Wendy too. We'll form our own little Scooby Doo gang and ride right into the police station.

**EMMIE.** Can you go after work?

**LOGAN.** I can't tonight.

I'm going to the movies with my friend.

Ron.

You want to come?

**EMMIE.** No.

Thanks, but – no.

**LOGAN.** Well, if you change your mind.

Ron is single.

**EMMIE.** Thank you.

**LOGAN.** He's a good guy.

**EMMIE.** I'll keep that in mind. Logan, do you promise we'll tell someone?

**LOGAN.** Yeah. Yeah.

Yeah, I promise.

I gotta stock.

EMMIE.  Logan.

LOGAN.  I said yeah okay!

I'll find you tomorrow.

*(He gives her a small hug.)*

*(LOGAN clocks in and leaves.)*

*(EMMIE clocks in and leaves.)*

## Six

*(The next day. In the warehouse.)*

*(**EMMIE** enters hauling two very large boxes of women's bras.)*

*(She unpacks and tags the bras. She puts each one on a plastic hanger after she's done, and puts each hanger on a rolling rack.)*

*(She unpacks and tags both boxes.)*

*(She sets down the tagger. Her wrist hurts from the repetitive motions.)*

*(She looks around the warehouse.)*

*(**WENDY** enters carrying two more boxes of bras.)*

WENDY.  Emmie. Sweetie. Take these.

*(Re: the bras on the rack.)* You done with these? Can I take them to the floor? I'm going to take them to the floor.

EMMIE.  Yup. Those are all set.

WENDY.  I'm still so sore about my New Year's plans. Dev said maybe we should have a little party tomorrow instead.

EMMIE.  That could be nice.

WENDY.  I haven't hosted in ages, but maybe we can have people bring snacks and drinks.

EMMIE.  Like a potluck.

WENDY.  Yes, exactly! Like a little potluck. Some deviled eggs. An M&M bowl. Maybe my peppermint punch.

EMMIE.  That sounds pretty great.

**WENDY.** You have plans? You want to come over for a New Year's potluck?

**EMMIE.** I have to work.

**WENDY.** I'm still so mad at myself for not inviting you over for Christmas.

**EMMIE.** Wendy.

**WENDY.** No, that's been haunting me for the past week! I don't know why I didn't. I'm sorry.

I let you spend it alone and I'm sorry. I'll make it up to you for New Year's!

> *(**LOGAN** enters.)*

**LOGAN.** Did you guys fucking hear?

**WENDY.** Hear what?

**LOGAN.** *(To **EMMIE**.)* I was looking for you.

**EMMIE.** What?

**LOGAN.** Okay. Otis drove by Gar's house last night, no car in the driveway, no one home. Otis tells Berry's that Gar's been five days no show –

**EMMIE.** So –

**LOGAN.** So Berry's terminated him.

**WENDY.** Oh jeez.

**LOGAN.** But here's the shit – they promoted Maxine because she handed in that personality test and they said they liked her "honesty."

**WENDY.** Oh my god.

**LOGAN.** She took the job. Max is the new Gar.

**WENDY.** She's never going to leave here.

**LOGAN.** Please. She complains more than anybody but she'll never quit.

**EMMIE.**  But.

What about Gar?

**LOGAN.**  I don't know.

> (**EMMIE** *looks at him.*)

Otis says maybe Gar hit big with poker. Skipped town.

**WENDY.**  Well. Then.

No news is good news.

**LOGAN.**  Yeah. Maybe it's fine.

**WENDY.**  It's fine.

**LOGAN.**  More than fine.

**WENDY.**  Maybe everything's good!

**EMMIE.**  Excuse me.

> (**EMMIE** *looks around the warehouse, looks down the aisles, and sees her future staring back at her.*)
>
> (*She leaves the warehouse.*)

Honey, you okay?

Emmie?

> (*A long moment.*)

**LOGAN.**  Yeah.

She's upset.

**WENDY.**  Well.

It is the strangest thing.

> (*A long moment.*)

I'm happy for Max. More money.

**LOGAN.** A little, not much, but. It might help her get out of that hotel.

**WENDY.** And good for us too, because she won't ride our asses.

**LOGAN.** Well, that's what we thought about Gar, so. Let's wait to get our hopes up.

Max wants to celebrate.

**WENDY.** Oh, just in time for New Year's!

**LOGAN.** I don't have any plans yet.

**WENDY.** We think we might have a potluck!

**LOGAN.** I kinda wanted to do karaoke.

**WENDY.** Well, oh, Emmie's working, maybe we'll go down to her bar! Ring in the new year with her and celebrate Maxine. That sounds fun, right?

**LOGAN.** Oh shit, yeah. I can practice some of my new stuff.

> *(They start heading for the door.* **WENDY** *pushes one of the bra rolling racks.)*
>
> *(***EMMIE** *enters the breakroom, steps onto a chair, pushes up one of the ceiling tiles and pulls her coat from a hiding spot.)*
>
> *(She takes her Walkman out of the pocket, sits down, puts on her headphones and plays her music.)*

**WENDY.** Help me with this.

**LOGAN.** Got it.

**WENDY.** Okay, this will be fun.

**LOGAN.** So much fun.

**WENDY.** Yeah, we need a little fun.